What Is Congress?

by Jill Abramson

illustrated by David Malan

Penguin Workshop

For Carl Hulse, great journalist,
great chronicler of the Congress—JA

For the republic—DM

PENGUIN WORKSHOP
An Imprint of Penguin Random House LLC, New York

Copyright © 2021 by Penguin Random House LLC. All rights reserved.
Published by Penguin Workshop, an imprint of Penguin Random House LLC, New York.
PENGUIN and PENGUIN WORKSHOP are trademarks of Penguin Books Ltd.
WHO HQ & Design is a registered trademark of Penguin Random House LLC.
Printed in the USA.

Visit us online at www.penguinrandomhouse.com.

Library of Congress Cataloging-in-Publication Data is available upon request.

ISBN 9780593223703 (paperback)   10 9 8 7 6 5 4 3 2 1
ISBN 9780593223710 (library binding)   10 9 8 7 6 5 4 3 2 1

Contents

Charles Sumner in the Senate

What Is Congress?

Senator Charles Sumner of Massachusetts was angry. Very angry. It was May 1856 when he stood up in the Senate. He was speaking out against a bill (a proposed law) that would let slavery spread in the United States. Northern states were very much against this.

One of the senators who wanted the bill passed was Andrew Butler. He was from South Carolina and a champion of slavery. Butler owned a plantation (a large farm) with sixty-four enslaved people working on it.

Butler was not at the Senate that day when Sumner spoke. Recently, Butler had suffered a stroke and had trouble walking and talking. So he didn't hear Sumner call him names. Nor did he see how Sumner was imitating how he spit when he talked and shuffled when he walked.

But a second cousin of Butler's, Preston Brooks, found out about it. He decided to strike back. Brooks was a member of Congress, too. He was in the House of Representatives.

Two days later, he and two friends crossed the marble hall from the House of Representatives to where the Senate met. Sumner sat at his desk, preparing to mail copies of his speech. Brooks

crept up behind him. He was carrying a cane with a heavy gold handle.

Before Sumner knew what was happening, Brooks began bashing Sumner over his head and body. Brooks beat him so savagely that the cane broke. Blood ran down Sumner's face. He couldn't see to get away. Brooks and his friend were gone before help came for Sumner.

It took the Massachusetts senator three years

to recover. Brooks was forced to resign from the House of Representatives, although his district voted him back into office.

Both Brooks and his cousin, Senator Butler of South Carolina, died shortly after the attack. As for Charles Sumner, he served many more years in the Senate and fought for equal rights for African Americans following the Civil War.

Over a history of almost two hundred and fifty years, there have been many fights in Congress over the laws it passes. But they have almost always been fights of words. None has ever been as bloody as what became known as "The Caning of Charles Sumner."

CHAPTER 1
In the Beginning

Before there was a president or even a United States of America, there was a Congress.

The thirteen American colonies first formed a Congress in 1774 to deal with the British government's so-called Intolerable Acts, which angered the colonists. As the situation worsened, they formed a second Congress in 1775, and then in 1776 broke away from Britain and started a war for independence. Congress became a kind of central government, a government over all the colonies. It would take care of shared needs, like paying an army to fight the war. But Congress was kept weak on purpose. The idea was to avoid anyone becoming like a king, drunk with power.

After the war, the new United States of America created a weak government. Each of the colonies was like its own little country, with its own money and leaders. The government was successful in dealing with some problems, but by 1786 it was clear that the country needed a stronger central or "federal" government with laws that all the states had to obey.

American troops fighting British soldiers
during the Revolutionary War

Still, many people hated the idea of their state giving up any power. So men from each state met in Philadelphia in 1787 to figure out how the new government would work. They met in total secrecy.

The signing of the US Constitution, 1789

Finally, and only after a lot of arguing, a written Constitution was approved. It set up a government with three branches: the legislative (Congress), the executive (the president), and the judicial (the courts). Power would be spread equally among the three branches.

Congress was the most important because it represented the people. It was set up to pass new laws.

To be fair to both large and small states, Congress was designed with two chambers. In the US Senate, there would be two members from each state, no matter its size. Members would be elected by their state governments to serve six-year terms. However, in the US House of Representatives, the number of members from each state would be based on its population. And members would be elected every two years.

Like a cup of tea, the Senate with its longer terms was supposed to be a "cooling saucer" for the hot tea that sometimes poured out of the House, where there was more turnover.

It is not a perfect system. Like the country it represents, the US Congress has not always been a cozy tea party. However, democracy has survived for more than 230 years. Other countries have tried to set up a similar government but none has lasted as long as ours.

Most and Fewest

As of 2020, in a country with more than 330 million people, there were 435 people in the House of Representatives. California had the largest number—fifty-three—because it had the most people living in it. Seven states had so few people, they only got to elect one member in the House. Those states were Alaska, Delaware, Montana, North Dakota, South Dakota, Vermont, and Wyoming.

53

California

1

Vermont

CHAPTER 2
Capital vs. Capitol

Originally, the men who wrote the Constitution could not even agree where the Congress should meet. The northern states wanted New York City or Philadelphia, while the southern states wanted the center of government to be in their region. Finally, in a compromise, a brand-new city was built: Washington, DC. It was then in the middle of the new country. It would be the capital (capital with an *A*) of the whole country. And that's where the Congress still meets, in a huge, domed building called the Capitol (with an *O*).

The majestic building faces the Washington Monument and Lincoln Memorial. It is designed to resemble buildings from ancient Greece and Rome where democracy first flourished.

The Capitol was built in stages and rebuilt several times. Its famous dome wasn't completed until 1863. In a photo of President Abraham Lincoln's first inauguration, the iron skeleton of the dome can be seen.

Below the dome is the Capitol rotunda, a central circular area. Before burial, the bodies of some of the most famous leaders of the United States have lain in state in the rotunda so citizens could come and pay their respects. Two floors below the rotunda there is an empty tomb. It was designed to hold George Washington's coffin.

The Capitol Building during the inauguration of Abraham Lincoln, 1861

But it's empty because Washington preferred to be buried at his home in Virginia.

The rotunda connects the southern part of the building, where the House of Representatives meets, with the northern side, which houses the

Capitol Building rotunda

The US Senate chamber

Senate. Above those chambers are galleries for visitors. Visitors are often surprised by how small the Senate chamber is and how close the wooden desks are to each other. In both the chambers for the House and for the Senate, the desks are arranged in a semicircle, divided by political party.

There are some interesting customs and traditions in Congress. In the Senate, for instance, the senator who sits closest to the door has "the candy desk." That senator must keep a drawer full of candy for hungry senators to grab as they come in and out of the chamber.

The Senate also has a fancy dining room, where a special bean soup is served every day.

Some of the customs seem very old-fashioned. Senators cannot address each other by name but must refer to each other as "The Gentleman from Virginia," or "The Gentlelady from Maine." Hats are not allowed in the House, and women senators who wear pants must also wear jackets. House members are also forbidden to spit when someone is giving a speech they don't like!

While important debates and votes take place in the chambers, most of the Congress members' work gets done in office buildings that flank the Capitol. The members of Congress who have served the longest get the best offices, those nearest the Capitol.

What do some members of Congress consider the best office perk of all?

Everyone is allowed to bring dogs to their office.

Ghosts in Congress?

During the Civil War (1861–1865), the Capitol was turned into a hospital for soldiers fighting for the North. Some people say they have seen the ghost of a wounded soldier from those days wandering the halls of Congress.

CHAPTER 3
How It Works

Today, underground subways connect most of the Congressional office buildings to the Capitol so Congress members won't miss important votes.

Do they appear for every single vote?

No!

In fact, some members of Congress get a bad reputation with voters because they miss so many votes.

Each chamber has special powers. For example, the House originates all tax and spending bills—such as giving loans to small businesses who lost a lot of money because of the coronavirus epidemic that began in 2020.

The Senate alone decides whether or not to approve the president's most important advisers (his Cabinet) and also to approve the people the president wants to be federal judges and on the Supreme Court.

For a law to pass, both chambers must approve it—and in exactly the same form. If there is a tie in the Senate, the vice president gets the tie-breaking vote.

After an election, whichever party wins a majority of seats in each chamber gets to call most of the shots. Members of the party in the minority often feel discouraged and powerless.

In the House of Representatives, the majority party chooses the Speaker, the most powerful member of Congress. In 2007, for the very first time, a woman became Speaker of the House— Nancy Pelosi from California. In fact, the Speaker of the House is next in line to become president if both the president and vice president die in office. (So far, that has never happened.)

In the Senate, whichever party has won a majority (that means at least fifty-one out of one hundred senators) picks a Senate majority leader. This, too, is an incredibly powerful position.

Could You Serve in Congress?

To serve, senators have to be at least thirty years old and have been a citizen of the United States for the last nine years. Each representative in the House must be at least twenty-five years old and be a US citizen for the past seven years. Senators and representatives must both live in the state they represent.

John F. Kennedy: Age 36, sworn into the Senate in 1953

People in the House or the Senate can stay in office as long as they keep getting elected. The president, however, can only be elected to two four-year terms.

Alexandria Ocasio-Cortez: Age 29, sworn into the House in 2019

Sometimes Congress gets a lot done, passing many important laws. That happens when the president belongs to the same political party that has a majority in both the House and the Senate. When one party controls the House and the other party controls the Senate, the government can sometimes almost come to a standstill.

For example, after the 2018 Congressional elections, Democrats won a majority of the House. Once again, Nancy Pelosi became Speaker. But Republicans still controlled the Senate.

The two parties had very different ideas about what kind of laws should be passed.

Republican Mitch McConnell of Kentucky was the Senate majority leader then. He liked the fact that he was known as the Grim Reaper (another name for Death). He got the nickname because he killed so many proposals sent to the Senate from the House. He didn't even let them be discussed, much less come to a vote.

Mitch McConnell

Also, remember that even after both the House and Senate have passed a bill, it must be signed by the president before it becomes law. The president can veto the bill. Does that end it? No. By a two-thirds vote, each chamber can override the president's veto. This happens very rarely. Then, too, there is also something called a pocket veto. It means that the president doesn't sign or veto a bill. It is as if he's just keeping it in his pocket. He waits until Congress is no longer in session and then the bill dies.

Pretty tricky, huh?

But if Congress stays in session, the bill becomes law after ten days whether the president signs it or not.

CHAPTER 4
Trouble from the Start

By the early decades of the nineteenth century, many of the Founders who fought in the Revolution and wrote the Constitution had died. A new generation of leaders in Congress had to step into their shoes. They were giant shoes to fill.

The Constitution had resolved many issues, but not the question of slavery. The pro-slavery Southern states said it was the right of each state whether or not to permit slavery. Northern states said no—the federal government had to end it everywhere in the country. Pure and simple, slavery was wrong. African Americans were human beings, not property that could be bought and sold. The biggest challenge in Congress was just holding the North and South together.

Enslaved people working in cotton fields

The United States was growing quickly beyond its thirteen original states. Political parties were becoming stronger, too. Both factors made reaching compromises more difficult.

The fight over slavery worsened when Missouri was about to become a state. Would it allow slavery or not?

Louisiana Purchase of 1803

After the Louisiana Purchase of 1803, the United States was no longer just the North and South. It was also the great big West. The country almost doubled in size. New states were carved out. The purchase included the land that today is Arkansas, Iowa, Missouri, Nebraska, and Oklahoma, as well as most of Louisiana, North Dakota, South Dakota, Kansas, Colorado, Wyoming, Montana, and Minnesota.

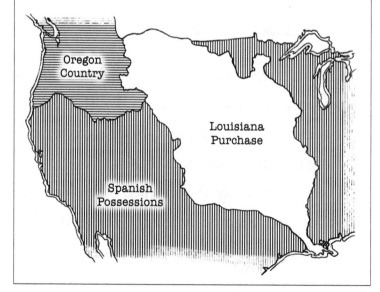

Henry Clay of Kentucky was the master dealmaker of Congress in this era. He served at different times in both the House and Senate.

He was a man who loved gambling and horses. But most of all he loved his country and did everything he could to keep the states united.

Clay thought of a way to settle—at least, for the time being—the fight over new states and slavery. He put together a law called the Missouri Compromise.

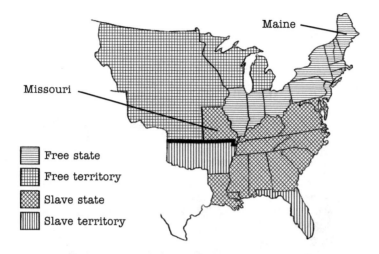

Maine

Missouri

Free state
Free territory
Slave state
Slave territory

At this time, Maine was also becoming a state. In Clay's law, slavery would be outlawed in Maine but in Missouri it would be permitted. This way there would be a balance—twelve states allowing slavery and twelve that didn't. The bill also created a line on Missouri's southern border. Above the line all new states would be free. Below the line, slavery could continue.

Clay tried to win the presidency five times but never won. Still, he had a long and great career in Congress and won the title "The Great Compromiser."

Thirty years after the Missouri Compromise, "The Great Compromiser" was needed again. In 1850, the fight over slavery flared up once more, only worse this time. Clay was able, just barely, to forge another agreement that kept the country together.

Henry Clay's fiercest opponent in the Senate was John Calhoun of South Carolina. Tall and thin, Calhoun was called the Cast-Iron Man in Congress because of how unbending he was on issues. He was a "states righter"—he wanted the South and slavery to be left alone.

John Calhoun

Calhoun argued that the Constitution allowed states opposing certain federal laws to disobey them. Calhoun was already talking about states leaving the union. Clay's compromises ended up only postponing the inevitable.

The footsteps of war could be plainly heard in the marble halls of Congress.

CHAPTER 5
Breaking Away

Abraham Lincoln is one of the best loved presidents in American history. However, he never had much of a career in Congress. He served one term as a House member from Illinois. And each of the two times he ran for Senate from Illinois he lost.

Yet in 1860 Lincoln managed to win the presidency in a very close four-way race. The South hated him because he was a Republican who had opposed the spread of slavery. By 1860, there were four million Black people living in bondage.

Even if Henry Clay had still been alive (he died in 1852), it is doubtful that he could have found a way for the Southern members of Congress to accept Lincoln.

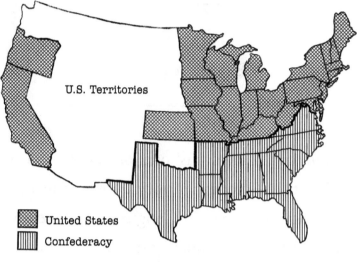

United States in 1861

Just weeks after Lincoln's election on November 6, 1860, South Carolina seceded—broke away—from the Union, on December 20. Mississippi and five other slaveholding states seceded even before Lincoln took office in March 1861. Soon a total of eleven states formed a new country—the Confederate States of America. And in April 1861, the first shots of the Civil War were fired at Fort Sumter in South Carolina. All those years of compromises in Congress had only postponed the breakup of the United States.

The eleven states of the Confederacy created their own government and had a new flag. A Confederate Congress met and wrote its own pro-slavery Constitution. It elected Jefferson Davis as president. (He had been a US senator before the war.) Missouri and Kentucky also joined the Confederacy by the end of 1861.

1861 flag of the Confederate States of America

With the Southern representatives and senators suddenly gone, the US Congress was much smaller. It had Republican majorities in both the House of Representatives and the

Senate. In both chambers, there was a powerful group called the Radical Republicans. They wanted slavery abolished everywhere in the United States. They viewed ending slavery as a moral issue. A big challenge for President Lincoln, who was not one of the Radical Republicans, was keeping those in Congress who were in line.

In the House, Pennsylvania's Thaddeus Stevens was the anti-slavery leader. He believed so strongly in equal rights for Black people that at the end of his life, he refused to be buried in a cemetery for white people only. On his tombstone, he had it written that equality was what he had fought for all his life.

Thaddeus Stevens

Thaddeus Stevens's grave site

Stevens favored punishing the South by taking away plantations from their owners and giving the land to freed Black people.

In the Senate, Charles Sumner of Massachusetts—the man who was beaten with a cane—was the leading Radical Republican.

Lincoln needed a big army if the North was going to win the Civil War. So Congress passed the first bill for a mandatory military draft.

(Mandatory means something you have to do.) Before this, young men didn't have to become soldiers. It was a volunteer army.

The Union Army had 600,000 soldiers by 1863. The Northern forces outnumbered the Confederates two to one. Also, by the end of the war there were more than 198,000 Black troops fighting for the North.

Clothing, feeding, housing, and arming all those soldiers cost a huge amount of money. So where did the money come from? From taxes. Only Congress had the power to raise taxes. During the Civil War, it passed the first income tax ever to pay for the Union Army's expenses.

The Congress in Washington, DC, also passed something called the Confiscation Act in 1862. It allowed the North to seize rebel property of people in the South. "Property" included enslaved people, and some of them, newly freed, immediately volunteered in the Union Army.

Some members of Congress lost sons in the war. One senator, Edward Dickinson Baker of Oregon, enlisted. Before heading off to war, he returned to the Senate proudly wearing his Union uniform. He was killed in the Battle of Ball's Bluff less than three months later.

Ending slavery required both the House and Senate to agree to change the Constitution. They could do this by passing the Thirteenth Amendment. (An amendment means to change or add something to a document.) A two-thirds majority was needed in both chambers. It passed easily in the Senate. However, in the House, everyone knew it would be much harder. They held their breath as the ayes and nays were counted. In the end, there were seven more votes than needed.

The Thirteenth Amendment became law in December 1865 after approval by the states. This ended slavery in the United States forever. The Civil War had ended in April of 1865. The war had raged for four years and

was by far the bloodiest in US history. It is estimated that as many as 750,000 soldiers died. The North had won. But the question now was, could a nation, once broken, be put back together?

Congress cheers after Thirteenth Amendment passes in the House

CHAPTER 6
Reconstruction

Sadly, Abraham Lincoln did not live to see the country reunited. On April 14, 1865, he was shot while at a theater in Washington, DC, and died the following morning. His assassin was a Southern sympathizer, an actor named John Wilkes Booth.

US Capitol dome under construction, 1864

Library of Congress/Corbis Historical/VCG/Getty Images

Senator Charles Sumner

Hiram Revels, the first African American US senator

The House impeachment managers, 1868

Jeannette Rankin, the first woman elected to the
US House of Representatives

Senator Joe McCarthy at a Senate Judiciary Committee hearing, 1950s

The opening session of the Watergate hearings, 1973

Nancy Pelosi after being elected as the first woman
Speaker of the House, 2007

Senator Mitch McConnell, 2009

Nancy Pelosi talking about the proposed
Affordable Health Care for America Act, 2009

Republican House Representative Louie Gohmert at a Tea Party rally, 2015

The female House Democratic members of the 116th Congress, 2019

Democratic congresswomen dressed in white to honor the
women's suffrage movement at the Presidential State of the Union, 2019

Impeachment hearing of President Donald Trump, 2020

Visitors touring the US Capitol Building, 2017

Senate Majority Leader Mitch McConnell walking to
the Senate chamber during the COVID-19 pandemic, 2020

Lincoln's vice president, Andrew Johnson, was sworn in as president. It fell to him to try to put the country back together. To reconstruct it. That's why this period is called Reconstruction. It lasted from 1866 to 1877.

Andrew Johnson

To say it very plainly, Andrew Johnson was a bad president. He had been a senator before becoming Lincoln's running mate in the 1864 election. Although he was against the South seceding, Johnson was not against slavery. So why had Lincoln chosen him?

It was because Johnson was from Tennessee, a state in the South. In late 1864, the North was close to winning the war. It was also a presidential election year. Lincoln thought picking a running mate from Tennessee might help heal the wounds of the war after the Southern states were back in the Union.

Lincoln had talked of welcoming back the Southern states. Congress, however, with Radical Republicans in charge, passed four Reconstruction Acts. They created stiff rules for the Southern states to rejoin the Union. Former Confederates had to swear loyalty to the Union and agree to obey its laws. Georgia was the last to rejoin in 1870.

President Johnson tried to veto these laws, but Congress had enough votes—a two-thirds majority—to override (cancel) his veto. Northern troops remained in the South. This was to make sure the former Confederate states gave people who had been enslaved their rights as US citizens.

The most important right was the right to vote. In Congress, Thaddeus Stevens and his Republican allies passed what became the Fifteenth Amendment in 1869. It gave the right

Congress established the Freedmen's Bureau to help out
formerly enslaved people as well as poor white people

to vote to all newly freed Black men. Were Black
women included? No. No women—white or
Black—in the United States were allowed to vote
until 1920.

During Reconstruction, seventeen African
Americans were elected and served in the US
Congress. (More than six hundred more were
elected to the state legislatures, and hundreds

Joseph Rainey

more held local offices across the South.) The first African Americans were elected to Congress in 1870. Joseph Rainey of South Carolina was elected to the US House of Representatives.

Hiram Revels of Mississippi became the first Black US senator. A minister and former principal of a high school for Black students, Senator Revels helped get Black mechanics hired in the Washington Navy Yard. He also tried but failed to get integrated public schools in Washington, DC.

Was this the beginning of lasting change in the South and in Congress?

Unfortunately no.

Hiram Revels

CHAPTER 7
A Big Step Backward

The presence of Black members in Congress did not last long.

By the end of 1877, US troops were no longer policing the former Confederate states. After they left, the recent laws and amendments granting rights to Black people were much harder to enforce.

In the years right after the war, white groups like the Ku Klux Klan (KKK) formed. They terrorized Black people in the South so that they would not dare try to vote. The KKK would round up African Americans and lynch them. Lynching meant African Americans were murdered without a trial, usually by hanging.

Members of the Ku Klux Klan

Southern states began electing new members of Congress who were all white. And once US troops were gone, state governments in the South passed rules what were called Jim Crow laws. These laws continued segregation (keeping Black people away from white people) and took away any chance of Black people being treated equally.

Black people couldn't sit in the same train cars as white people. Black children couldn't go to school with white children. Restaurants had signs that read "For Whites Only."

In addition, although slavery had ended, a practice called involuntary servitude, or sharecropping, kept Black farmers working for almost no pay in fields owned by white people.

In Congress, the South tended to elect the same men over and over again. The longer they served, the more powerful they became. They could block any laws that they didn't like. And the laws they disliked the most were any that helped Black people gain civil rights.

The southern states' Jim Crow laws remained in effect until a Supreme Court ruling finally overturned them. But that didn't happen until 1954, almost eighty years after Reconstruction.

Reconstruction had held out the hope that African Americans would be treated as equal citizens. That did not happen. After 1901, there would not be another Black member of Congress for the next twenty-eight years. Since 1865, almost two thousand people have served in the US Senate. But only eleven have been Black.

The Radical Republicans in Congress weren't only fighting for the Reconstruction Acts. They were also fighting against President Johnson, who wanted to block these laws. Relations between the two branches of the government grew even worse after Johnson fired Secretary of War Edwin Stanton, in 1868.

Andrew Johnson with Edwin Stanton

Stanton had been appointed by Lincoln. He was popular with the Congress because he had helped the North win the Civil War. After his firing, Congress struck back. The House of Representatives voted to impeach Johnson—the first step in removing him. This had never happened before to a president. But in the Constitution, Congress was given the right to remove a president for abusing the power of his office.

First, the House of Representatives had to bring up charges and vote on them. In Johnson's case, the majority voted to uphold the charges that included firing Stanton. That meant Johnson was impeached. But he couldn't be removed from office unless a trial in the Senate found him guilty.

At the time, there were fifty-four senators—two from each of the twenty-seven states represented at the time. A two-thirds majority of them (thirty-six) had to vote guilty for Johnson to be thrown out of office. At the trial's end, the vote came down to thirty-five voting guilty and nineteen voting not guilty.

Andrew Johnson kept his job because of a single vote. This proved that the US system of government worked. There was no uprising in Congress because Johnson got to remain in office. Members stuck to the rules of the Constitution and the government went on.

Impeachment trial of Andrew Johnson

CHAPTER 8
Looking Out for Ordinary People

In the decades around the turn of the twentieth century, the United States again grew much larger. The economy shifted from agriculture to industry. Congress needed to pass laws to address the changes in the country. For the first time, Congress took responsibility for the welfare of American workers and consumers.

Some companies like Standard Oil, owned by John D. Rockefeller, had become so big that they were crushing smaller competitors. They were becoming nearly as powerful as the US government.

Many reporters—called "muckrakers"—pushed Congress to pass laws to control big businesses and pass new amendments to the Constitution.

This period of reform, called the Progressive Era, brought Congress more directly into the lives of everyday Americans.

The muckrakers exposed the dangerous working conditions in meatpacking plants, the corrupt business practices of railroads and oil companies, and the widespread use of child labor. In factories and coal mines, children as young as ten were working long hours in unsafe places instead of attending school. It was a time when the rich were getting richer, and the poor were getting poorer.

Robert La Follette

Congress suddenly sprang into action, prodded by Republican president Theodore Roosevelt and Wisconsin senator Robert ("Fighting Bob") La Follette. He championed anti-corruption laws and was an enemy of big businesses. Laws were passed that set up standards for the meatpacking, drug, and railroad industries.

Life for every American changed when Congress passed three important amendments to the Constitution. One gave Congress the right to collect money through a yearly federal income tax. Another amendment prohibited (outlawed) making and selling liquor. This was intended to reduce crime at a time when crooked politicians operated out of bars. But prohibition of alcohol actually had the opposite effect.

Congress outlaws the selling and making of liquor

It increased crime, as gangsters moved in to control illegal liquor sales and gang violence erupted in the cities. Prohibition, passed in 1919, was repealed (removed) with the Twenty-First Amendment in 1933.

Finally, in 1919, in a historic move, Congress passed the Nineteenth Amendment, giving women the right to vote. Even before that,

in 1916, Jeannette Rankin from Montana had become the first woman elected to Congress, serving in the House. Isn't it odd that a woman could be elected to Congress before women could vote? By 2021, 26 percent of the Senate and 27 percent of the House was female.

Jeannette Rankin

CHAPTER 9
Power Shifts to the President

All during the 1920s, it seemed like the good times would go on forever. Many ordinary Americans were more well-off. They bought stocks in companies, and for years they saw the value of their stocks rise. Then in 1929, the stock market crashed. Many people lost all their money overnight. Businesses closed. Factories slowed to a halt and fired their workers.

Hoovervilles

Poverty became so widespread that there were soup kitchens and breadlines to feed starving people. In many cities, there were people living in tents and hovels, called Hoovervilles. These communities got their name from the president, Herbert Hoover.

The Depression's horrors were not confined to the cities. There were terrible dry spells in the South and Southwest, and farmers couldn't plant their crops. Dust storms made the air so thick that people could not see in front of them. Many people packed up their belongings and went west to California, often on rickety carts pulled by horses.

The economy became so bad that by 1932, thirteen million people were unemployed.

Then along came Franklin Delano Roosevelt (FDR) who promised to get the country moving again. By pledging a "New Deal," he won the presidential election of 1932 in a landslide.

In his inaugural address, Roosevelt famously said, "The only thing we have to fear is fear itself." But he couldn't fight the Depression or enact the New Deal without Congress.

On his very first day as president, Roosevelt sent Congress a package of proposals to help restart the economy. He declared a four-day bank holiday. That meant closing banks for four days to stop panicked people from withdrawing all of their money.

Congress went from being frozen to dancing to Roosevelt's tune. The executive branch was leading the way and the legislative branch was following. This began a period in which the power of the president grew mightily.

Thirteen major laws that FDR sent to Congress were passed right away. One, the Emergency Banking Relief Act, took just eight hours to pass—that had never happened before.

The most famous of these laws created Social Security, the program that still provides money as a safety net for the elderly. Also, workers out of a job could now collect unemployment insurance. Through another program, the National Industrial Recovery Act, many were also given jobs paid for by the government where they built dams and roads and constructed public buildings.

Workers constructing the Hoover Dam

Not everyone was happy about Congressional power weakening. In fact, the US Supreme Court overturned some of the laws FDR had Congress pass.

FDR was elected president four times. (No other president before had served more than two terms.) After FDR's death, Congress passed a Constitutional amendment that limited future presidents to two elected terms. Congress was making sure it kept its powers.

Congress, for instance, has the sole power to declare war, even though the president always takes the lead in dealing with leaders from other countries. This is what's called foreign policy.

In 1939, Roosevelt wanted the United States to join Britain, France, and Russia in fighting Nazi Germany and Adolf Hitler, who was trying to take over Europe. However, members of Congress called "isolationists" stopped him. Among them were senators Arthur Vandenberg and Robert Taft. Isolationists believed that because the war was being fought so far away, it was not a danger to the United States.

Arthur Vandenberg

Robert Taft

Then everything changed in December 1941 when the Japanese bombed the American naval base at Pearl Harbor, in Hawaii. (Japan was on Germany's side in the war.)

Attack on Pearl Harbor, 1941

Right away Congress approved what Roosevelt wanted—joining the war. The only member of Congress to vote against entering World War II was Jeannette Rankin. (She had been elected again to the House of Representatives in 1940.) "As a woman I can't go to war," she said, "and I refuse to send anyone else." After casting her lone no vote, Rankin was hissed and booed and mobbed by journalists, forcing her to hide "like a cornered rabbit" in a Capitol phone booth.

Although there were opponents to FDR's domestic policies in the House and Senate, Congress followed Roosevelt's lead because he was so popular with the people. Like Lincoln, he was a leader who spoke to the soul of the country. FDR and Congress saved America during the Depression and united everyone during the four years of World War II.

CHAPTER 10
The Red Scare

The years right after World War II marked one of the most shameful chapters in the history of Congress. Members were unfairly jailing citizens whom they believed were trying to bring down America. It all had to do with worry about the spread of Communism.

Communist Russia had been a US ally in fighting Hitler during the war. (Its formal name was the Union of Socialist Soviet Republics, or USSR.) The USSR lost more lives during the war than any other country, an astounding twenty million people. However, soon after the war was over, Russia and the United States became enemies in what was called the "Cold War." No actual battles were fought between them directly.

Communism

Communism is a very different kind of government from that of the United States. Under Communism, the government owns and controls businesses and land. In return, it provides citizens with the basics they need in life—housing, food, education, and jobs. One party rules—the Communist Party. It has all the power. People must obey party leaders.

Vladimir Lenin, former leader of USSR

But the United States feared that Russia was trying to spread Communism and become the number one world superpower.

Some members of Congress deliberately fanned a "Red Scare." (The Communist flag was red, and so in America, Communists were known as Reds.)

The Red Scare was used to convince Americans that Communism was spreading within the United States, threatening democracy. In the House of Representatives, the House Un-American Activities Committee (HUAC) began investigating supposed Communists who worked in the movie industry.

J. Parnell Thomas

HUAC's chairman after the war, J. Parnell Thomas of New Jersey, brought his committee out to Hollywood in May 1947 to summon directors, producers, and screenwriters. This was a publicity stunt. (He wanted newspapers to cover what he was doing.) Ten industry leaders, however, refused to do what Thomas wanted and "name names" of other Communists. So they were charged with contempt of Congress, fined, and sent to prison for a year. Afterward, anyone else who didn't "name names" to Thomas's committee went on a blacklist. That meant no one working in Hollywood would hire them.

Protesters against the HUAC

Joe McCarthy

In the Senate, anti-Communist frenzy was whipped up by an ambitious, unscrupulous senator from Wisconsin— Joe McCarthy. He held up a stack of papers and claimed to have the names of hundreds of Communists working inside the US government on behalf of Russia. He didn't; it was all a lie.

Like Thomas, he called witnesses before his committee not only to attack them but to force them to tell who else was Communist. But in 1954, McCarthy went too far when he started accusing people serving in the US army.

McCarthy's Senate hearings were broadcast on the new television networks. Americans began to see for themselves that he was a demagogue.

A demagogue is a politician who appeals to people's prejudices and worst fears.

Attacking the army was McCarthy's undoing because American armed forces were held in high regard. They had recently helped win the war against Germany and Japan.

Shaking his head, Joseph Welch, who was

Joseph Welch

the lawyer representing the army, famously said to McCarthy, "You've done enough. Have you no sense of decency, sir?"

Before Thomas and McCarthy were done, they had ruined the lives of many people who lost their jobs because of these accusations. People were forced to sign "loyalty oaths" to America to prove they were not Communists. Actually, the people who refused to sign or testify were living up to the First Amendment of the Constitution. It guarantees free speech to everyone—meaning they can think whatever they want. It also protects the right to "free association"—meaning people can gather together and share their views.

In the end, Thomas and McCarthy were the

ones who disgraced democracy. McCarthy was censured by the Senate in 1954. Censure means calling out the disgraceful things a politician has done.

McCarthy died of alcoholism three years after he was censured. Thomas came to a bad end, too. He was sent to prison for corruption. Thomas ended up serving time in the very same prison as two members of the Hollywood Ten.

Punishments

Censure is one of the ways that Congress can punish its own members under the Constitution. Other punishments include reprimand, a less serious charge than censure, and expulsion—being kicked out of office. These penalties can be applied to members of Congress who "act dishonorably" or behave in a disorderly manner. Only fifteen senators and five members of the House have been

expelled since 1789. It takes a vote of two-thirds of each chamber to approve these rare punishments. Senators who are censured can remain in office but can't be the chairman of any congressional committee.

In 1797, William Blount became the first senator recommended for expulsion from Congress

CHAPTER 11
A Fairer America

In 1957, over the stiff objections of southern members, Congress passed the first Civil Rights Act since Reconstruction. It was a weak bill. Nevertheless, South Carolina senator Strom Thurmond, who hated integration, tried to block it. The method he used was something called a filibuster. It means making a speech in Congress that prevents a vote on a law from happening.

Strom Thurmond

Thurmond gave the longest individual speech in Senate history. He talked continuously for twenty-four hours and eighteen minutes. Eventually, Thurmond's filibuster ended and the Senate passed the bill.

This was a start. Over the next few years, the civil rights movement gained force in the country. The times were changing and Congress had to keep up.

In 1963, the assassination of President John F. Kennedy brought Lyndon Johnson, who had been vice president, into the White House. Johnson was a Texan who'd grown up in poverty to become a seasoned leader of Congress. He was a member of the House of Representatives and later served as Senate majority leader. He knew where all the levers of power were in Congress and how to pull them in order to get things done. In the Senate, he was famous for "the Johnson Treatment," using a mixture of charm and fear to make other senators vote his way.

Senate Majority Leader Lyndon Johnson persuading a politician

Because of these skills, once Johnson became president he was able to get Congress to pass more laws to help the people than any president since FDR. In the mid-1960s, Congress finally passed a strong civil rights bill, a voting rights act to ensure Black people had their voice in elections, and a fair housing law which made it illegal for neighborhoods to keep out Black homeowners.

President Lyndon Johnson signs the Civil Rights Act of 1964

At the signing, Martin Luther King Jr., the civil rights leader, was present as well as John Lewis, a future representative from Georgia who served in Congress from 1986 until his death in 2020.

John Lewis

And then there was Medicare, the program that still pays for the medical care of the elderly and some people with disabilities. Johnson wanted to make America into what he called "The Great Society." These programs were aimed at achieving just that, turning the United States into a fair place for all its citizens.

Unfortunately, a time that was meant to bring progress ended up bitterly dividing the country. It was because of a long war the United States fought in a small country in Southeast Asia . . . Vietnam.

CHAPTER 12
Watergate

The United States was divided in Congress. Hawks, who were for the Vietnam War, and doves, who were against it, were unable to work together to settle the fighting in Southeast Asia. (The war didn't end until 1975; almost 55,000 American soldiers lost their lives, and Vietnam did in the end become a Communist country.)

Oddly enough, a major scandal that shook the nation actually brought Republicans and Democrats in Congress together.

Richard Nixon followed Lyndon Johnson as president in 1968. Smart and hardworking, Nixon was also quick to smear opponents with lies and willing to use dirty tricks to win elections.

In 1972, Nixon ran for reelection and won in a landslide. Nixon hadn't needed to do anything crooked, but he did.

Well before the presidential election, Nixon okayed a burglary of the Democratic Party headquarters at the Watergate complex (a group of buildings) in Washington, DC. The goal was for the burglars to find out how the Democrats were planning to campaign against Nixon. The president and his aides were also accused of lying in order to cover up the crime.

Watergate complex

To guard against the abuse of power, the Constitution gives each branch of government oversight over the other two. So when the burglary happened, Congress was able to investigate.

At the beginning of the Watergate scandal, Republicans in Congress defended President Nixon because of party loyalty. But that evaporated after witness accounts of many illegal acts inside the White House piled up. The chairman of the Senate Watergate hearings was an old, gravelly-voiced North Carolina Democrat,

Sam Ervin. He was trusted by senators from both parties. They saw he was carrying out the duty of Congress to hold the president to the law. (The House of Representatives had its own Watergate committee.)

The Senate Watergate hearings were televised and the country was glued to them. At one hearing, Senator Howard Baker Jr., a Republican from Tennessee, asked the famous question, "What did the president know and when did he know it?"

Sam Ervin presiding over the
Senate Watergate Committee hearings

One of the witnesses who worked in the White House revealed that President Nixon taped all of his White House conversations. Right away, Congress demanded the tapes to see if they contained evidence about the Watergate burglary.

President Nixon refused to hand over the tapes. He claimed as president he had "executive privilege." This meant the president had the right to keep certain matters like the tapes private. Ervin's committee voted unanimously to sue the president—something no Congressional committee had ever done in the history of the country.

In July 1974, the US Supreme Court ruled that Nixon had to turn over the tapes. The president was

President Nixon's tape recorder

not above the law. And, yes, the tapes did indeed show evidence of Nixon's criminal involvement in Watergate. That very same day, the House Judiciary Committee was to start debating whether to impeach Nixon.

A small group of senators and House members went to the White House to talk to President Nixon. They told him he had lost the support of his own party. The leader of the group was a Republican, Senator Barry Goldwater, who had once been loyal to Nixon.

Richard Nixon realized his presidency was doomed. He would have to give up the job that he had worked for all his life. The next day, August 8, 1974, he became the first US president ever to resign.

CHAPTER 13
Dividing Lines

The kind of bipartisanship seen during the Watergate scandal seems unthinkable in Congress today. (Bipartisanship means opposing parties working together.) Over the past twenty-five years, Congress has become deeply divided along party lines—more perhaps than at any time since the years right before the Civil War. Today, even friendships between Democrat and Republican leaders have become rare.

Control of Congress has shifted from Democrats to Republicans and back again several times, making it more and more difficult for Congress to pass big proposals. Or laws would get passed by one Congress and then get rolled back by a later Congress.

In 1994, when Democrat Bill Clinton was president, voters elected droves of Republicans as House members. It was called "The Republican Revolution." For the first time in four decades, Republicans were in the House majority. They picked a fiery conservative, Newt Gingrich of Georgia, to be Speaker of the House.

Like most Republicans in the twentieth century, Gingrich believed the federal government was too big. It had too much involvement in people's lives, helping them out when they should be helping themselves. He pushed through bills that cut taxes and government programs like welfare.

Newt Gingrich

Gingrich also had President Clinton impeached for lying under oath about an affair with a young White House aide. But as with Andrew Johnson's trial more than one hundred years earlier, the Senate voted for Clinton to remain in office.

Voters thought Gingrich and the Republicans had gone too far with impeachment, so the Democrats were returned to power in the 1998 Congressional elections. As for Newt Gingrich, he resigned from the speakership after it became public that he had been having an affair of his own with a young aide.

After the 9/11 attacks, for a brief time there was bipartisanship again—now over ways to protect the country against other terrorists.

Congress passed laws as part of the "War on Terror." These bills let federal agencies investigate and imprison suspected terrorists. It approved new government spying powers, too, which were met with criticism. The Senate—Democrats and Republicans alike—voted to approve a much-debated war against Iraq. There had been no connection between Iraq and 9/11, and with time it became clear that the costly war had been a mistake.

President Barack Obama signs the Affordable Care Act

The only big domestic program that Congress has passed in recent years is the Affordable Care Act. That's a program in which the government provides cheap health insurance to Americans. It is often called Obamacare because it was sent to Congress by President Barack Obama, and Democratic Speaker Pelosi was instrumental in getting it passed. Republicans were not at all in favor of it. They thought the program was too expensive and was forcing people to buy health insurance.

Almost right away there was an angry uprising among Republican voters from the South and the middle of the country. They called themselves "The Tea Party" and were dead set against big government programs like Obamacare. They elected members to Congress and in 2017 Obamacare was almost repealed. It was saved by a single vote that came from a Republican senator who broke ranks—John McCain of Arizona.

Donald Trump

This same group of angry voters grew and banded behind the real-estate tycoon and reality-TV star Donald Trump. He ran for president as a Republican in 2016 and won. He had never worked in government before, but that was exactly what many voters wanted.

In Congress, in 2017, both chambers had a Republican majority. They passed a big tax cut but it mostly benefited the rich. There was a lot of fighting over immigration laws. (President Trump wanted to build a wall along the border with Mexico to keep out undocumented immigrants;

Congress, however, did not approve all the money Trump wanted.) Still, the Senate did see to it that hundreds of President Trump's nominees for judges went through, including three new justices of the US Supreme Court. These judges all were conservative in their political outlook.

Not many Republican leaders in Congress had supported President Trump before his upset victory. However, Republicans in Congress grew very loyal to President Trump because of his popularity with certain voters.

After the 2018 Congressional elections, Democrats won back control of the House of Representatives with a record number of women and Black people elected as new members. Nancy Pelosi reclaimed her job as Speaker of the House. However, the Senate still had a Republican majority. The two chambers were unable to work together and the result was that no major bills were passed.

Democratic congresswomen wore white to
President Trump's State of the Union address, 2019.

Once again, a president was impeached by the House. It happened at the end of 2019. Trump was accused of asking a foreign country to help tilt the 2020 election in his favor by digging up dirt on Joe Biden, his Democratic rival for the presidency. And once again, the Senate acquitted a president, so Trump remained in office.

Then in January 2021, the House impeached him again! This had never happened before in American history.

Why was Trump impeached a second time?

He incited (encouraged) thousands of his supporters to storm the Capitol. Trump was furious because Joe Biden had won the 2020 election. President Trump refused to accept the results, falsely claiming voter fraud.

So on January 6, 2021, a violent mob broke into the House and Senate chambers. They smashed windows and trashed offices. A police officer was beaten to death with a fire extinguisher.

Four other people died.

The Capitol Building was closed for hours. But that night, the Senate and House both came back to continue the work of a democracy.

Many people believe that Congress doesn't work anymore. Still, we are a nation of laws, and only Congress can make and pass laws that affect

the whole country. Our system of government is messy, but in times of crisis, Congress rises to the occasion.

At its best, Congress has changed the lives of Americans for the better. Being elected to Congress remains one of the most honored ways to serve the nation.

Timeline of Congress

1789 — The first US Congress meets in New York City

1793 — Breaking ground for the US Capitol begins

1800 — Congress moves from Philadelphia to Washington, DC

1861 — The Civil War begins

1865 — Congress passes the Thirteenth Amendment, which bans slavery

1868 — President Andrew Johnson is impeached by the House but acquitted in the Senate

1870 — Hiram Revels from Mississippi is seated as the first Black member of the US Senate

1877 — Reconstruction ends. State and local governments in the South begin enacting Jim Crow laws

1920 — Ratification of the Nineteenth Amendment giving women the right to vote

1957 — Passage of the Civil Rights Act of 1957

1964 — Congress passes the Civil Rights Act of 1964

2002 — Congress authorizes military force against Iraq

2010 — Congress passes the Affordable Care Act (Obamacare)

2017 — Senate Republicans fail to repeal the Affordable Care Act

2021 — A pro-Trump mob storms the Capitol. President Trump is impeached for the second time by Congress

Timeline of the World

1783 — The Treaty of Paris officially recognizes the United States as an independent country

1886 — The Statue of Liberty, a gift from France, takes its place in New York Harbor

1912 — The RMS *Titanic* sinks on its maiden voyage

1922 — British archaeologist Howard Carter discovers the tomb of the Egyptian pharaoh Tutankhamen

1939–1945 — World War II is fought

1957 — The USSR launches Sputnik 1, the first artificial satellite, into space

1964 — Beatlemania sweeps across America

1968 — Martin Luther King Jr. is assassinated in Memphis, Tennessee

1970 — The first Earth Day is celebrated

1986 — The US space shuttle *Challenger* explodes, killing all seven crew members

2009 — Barack Obama becomes the first African American president of the United States

2019 — Teenager Greta Thunberg becomes a world-famous activist for the environment

2020 — The COVID-19 pandemic spreads around the world

Bibliography

*Books for young readers

*Berstein, Richard B., and Jerome Agel. *The Congress. Into the Third Century.* New York: Walker and Company, 1988.

Bordewich, Fergus M. *The First Congress.* New York: Simon & Schuster, 2016.

Caro, Robert A. *Master of the Senate: The Years of Lyndon Johnson.* New York: Alfred A. Knopf, 2002.

Hofstadter, Richard. *The American Political Tradition and the Men Who Made It.* New York: Alfred A. Knopf, 1948.

Kennedy, John F. *Profiles in Courage.* New York: Harper and Brothers, 1956.

Redman, Eric. *The Dance of Legislation.* New York: Simon and Schuster, 1973.

*Ritchie, Donald A. *The Congress of the United States: A Student Companion*, 3rd ed. New York: Oxford University Press, 2006.

*Ritchie, Donald A. *The Senate.* New York: Chelsea House Publishers, 1988.

Websites

www.house.gov

www.senate.gov